M

NO

L

C

Counted Cross-Stitch Designs For All Seasons

Counted Cross-Stitch Designs For All Seasons

Jana Hauschild Lindberg

CHARLES SCRIBNER'S SONS   NEW YORK

Copyright © 1983 Jana Hauschild Lindberg

Library of Congress Cataloging in Publication Data

Lindberg, Jana Hauschild.
    Counted cross-stitch designs for all seasons.

    1. Cross-stitch—Patterns.   I. Title.
TT778.C76L56   1983   746.44   82-42669
ISBN 0-684-17883-4

1   3   5   7   9   11   13   15   17   19   Q/C   20   18   16   14   12   10   8   6   4   2

Printed in the United States of America.

Book design: H. Roberts Design

To John

CONTENTS

WINTER

PREFACE

I have always found cross stitch to be one of the simplest, most versatile, and most elegant needlecrafts. In creating the designs for this book, I wanted to show the many fresh ways cross stitch can be used to decorate the home throughout each season of the year. The projects also make ideal gifts for special occasions. In this age of mass production, we all look for ways to bring a personal touch to the things we give our family and friends. It is my hope that your cross-stitch embroideries will be treasured for many years, just as some of mine have. Recently, I was thrilled to find that a small tablecloth—my first endeavor, and not the most perfect piece of needlework—was still in daily use by my aunts, long after store-bought gifts had been forgotten.

The projects in *Counted Cross Stitch Designs for All Seasons* can be followed exactly, or you can stitch new designs by changing the colors, combining motifs from several projects, or using the motifs in different ways. I encourage you to experiment, to use your imagination to create embroideries that are uniquely yours. Perhaps you will discover gifts as a designer that you didn't know you had!

INTRODUCTION

MATERIALS

The designs in this book are created for counted cross stitch, an ancient technique that is very simple to learn and that requires few materials. You will need a fabric that is evenly woven, on which it is easy to count the threads (Figure 1). If you use a fabric that is not evenly woven, your embroidery will be distorted vertically or horizontally (Figures 2 and 3). Most of the designs in this book have been worked on linen that measures 25 threads per inch (10 threads per centimeter). You can select other types of fabric with different thread counts, but you may need to use more strands of embroidery yarn in the needle than are indicated in the instructions to cover the fabric completely. The formula on page 13 shows how to calculate the size of the finished piece if you use a fabric other than the one suggested.

Other supplies you will need are a blunt tapestry needle (#24 or #26); embroidery yarn (the graphs have been keyed to shades of DMC yarn throughout the book; you can substitute another brand by comparing its shades of yarn with the color plate of the design); an embroidery hoop; and a pair of sharp embroidery scissors, which is useful for cutting out mistakes. Some of the projects require brass or bamboo fittings, additional material for backing, and the like—this is indicated in the instructions for each design.

FIGURE 1

FIGURE 2

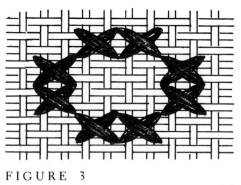

FIGURE 3

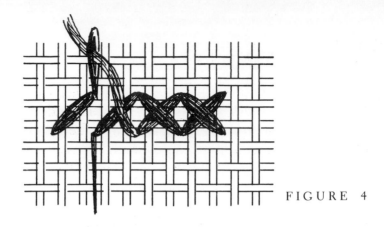

FIGURE 4

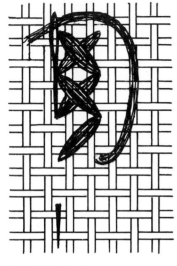

FIGURE 5

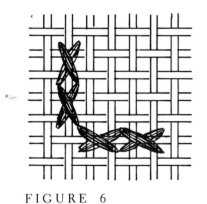

FIGURE 6

TECHNIQUE

Cross stitches are little X's that cover two threads horizontally and two vertically. All understitches are made in one direction and all the overstitches in the opposite direction (Figure 4). The Danish and American style is to begin understitches from left to right, crossing back from right to left; the British style is the reverse. It makes no difference, as long as you are consistent throughout the embroidery.

You can work all the bottom stitches first and then all the top stitches, or you can cross each stitch individually (more yarn will be used if you do the latter). For a vertical row one cross stitch wide, each stitch must be crossed individually (Figure 5).

When starting or ending a piece of yarn, do not tie a knot in it; the knot would show from the right side of the work. Start the first piece of yarn by leaving a tail long enough to thread back into the needle later on, after you have stitched a few rows. Then rethread the needle and weave the tail into the backs of several stitches. Start and fasten off subsequent pieces of yarn by weaving them into the backs of stitches in the same way. Clip the ends close with embroidery scissors, being careful not to cut any of the stitches.

In some places the designs call for half stitches, which are either worked over two threads horizontally and one vertically, or over one thread horizontally and two vertically (Figure 6). Three-quarter cross stitches are illustrated in Figure 7.

Backstitches are sewn over two threads, just as the cross stitches are, in the direction indicated on the graph (Figure 8).

FIGURE 7

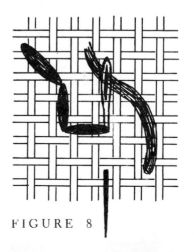

FIGURE 8

WORKING THE DESIGNS

Overcast the raw edges of the linen to prevent fraying. Find the center of the fabric by folding it in half in both directions and creasing it. Find the center of the design by following the arrows on the graph until they intersect. Directions on where to begin stitching each design are given with the project instructions. Be sure the fabric is oriented to match the design; you don't want to discover too late that you are stitching a vertical design on a horizontal piece of material.

Embroidery should proceed toward the sides and downward, never upward. To embroider the top half of a design that you have started in the middle, turn the work and the graph 180° (upside down); don't forget to turn the graph symbols as well. The slant of the stitches will then be the same throughout the embroidery. If you prefer to work downward from the top of the design, count up from the center. Every square on the graph is a full cross stitch on the fabric, so count two threads for each square.

To stitch the embroidery on a fabric other than the 25-count linen recommended in the instructions, calculate how large the finished piece will be according to this formula:

Multiply the piece's finished measurement (given in the instructions) by the number of threads per inch in the linen it is sewn on. Then divide that figure by the number of threads per inch in the fabric you want to sew on.

Thus, if a piece is 6 × 6″ on 25-count linen and you want to stitch it on a fabric with 18 threads to the inch, calculate as follows: 6 × 25 = 150 ÷ 18 = 8.3. The finished piece will be approximately 8¼ inches square. Remember when you are cutting fabric to allow a generous margin, 2 inches or so all around.

FINISHING

When the embroidery is finished, wash it in lukewarm water with mild soap. Rinse it well, adding a little vinegar to the last rinse. Do not wring. Roll the embroidery up in a towel and gently press out the excess water. Spread the piece right side down on your ironing board, cover it with a thin, slightly moistened cloth, and iron until both cloth and embroidery are dry.

Instructions for hemming the embroideries and for other finishing touches are given with each project.

✕✕Spring✕✕

✂✂ WALLHANGING WITH YELLOW TULIPS

See Plate 1.

Finished size: 11 × 13″ (28 × 32 cm.)
Cutting size: 16 × 20″ (40 × 50 cm.)

Materials

Linen with 25 threads/in. (10/cm.)
DMC embroidery yarn, one skein of each color
One brass or bamboo fitting, approximately 12″ (30 cm.)

Instructions

Find the center of the fabric and of the design. Begin embroidering at the center, using 2 strands of yarn in the needle. Press the finished work. To mount as a wallhanging, fold the surplus material at the two long sides to the back and sew with small stitches. Then make a casing by folding over 20 threads at the top and bottom edges and sewing with small stitches. Insert a brass or bamboo fitting. To mount as a picture, center the embroidery over a piece of white ragboard. Turn the margins to the back and lace them together with button thread from top to bottom and from side to side. The embroidery is now ready to be framed.

DMC yarn

Symbol	Code	Color
●	3346	dark green
⊠	3347	medium green
◪	471	light green
C	472	lightest green
◹	420	brown
⊠	832	gold
V	734	yellow-green
6	783	dark gold
▼	972	orange
⋈	444	dark yellow
Z	307	medium yellow
•	445	light yellow
◣	798	dark blue
⫽	799	medium blue

WALLHANGING WITH YELLOW TULIPS *(top part of design)*

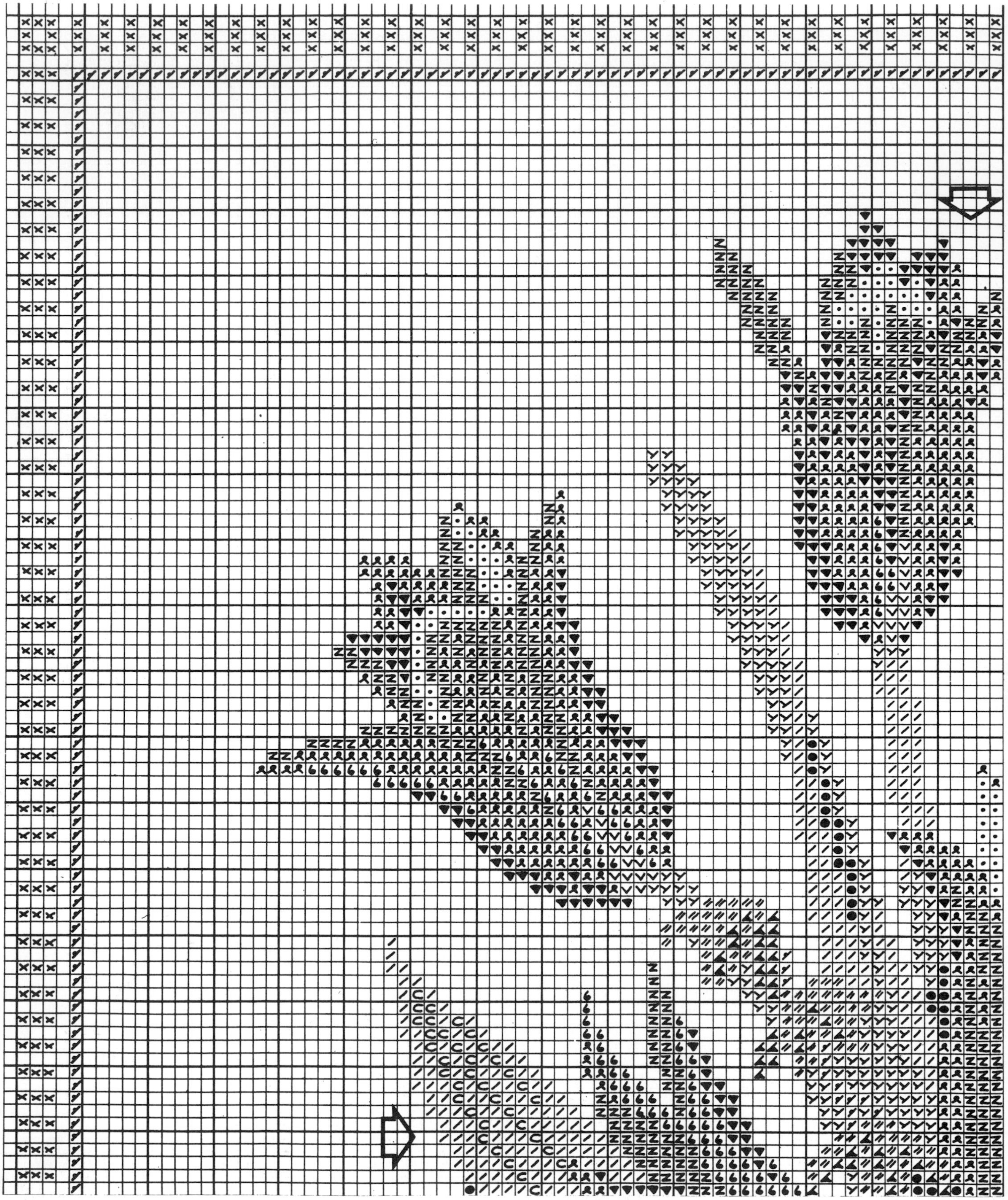

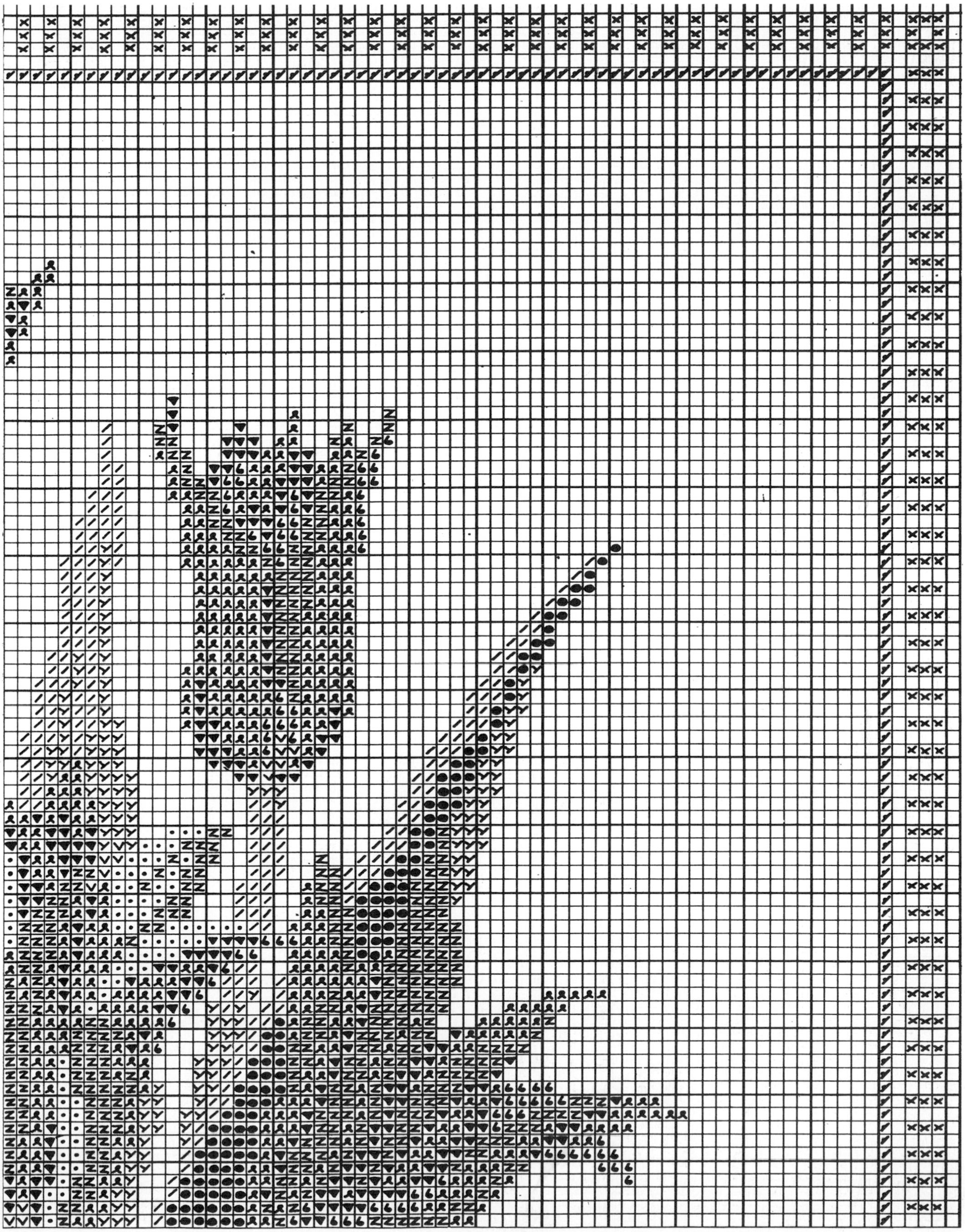

WALLHANGING WITH YELLOW TULIPS *(bottom part of design)*

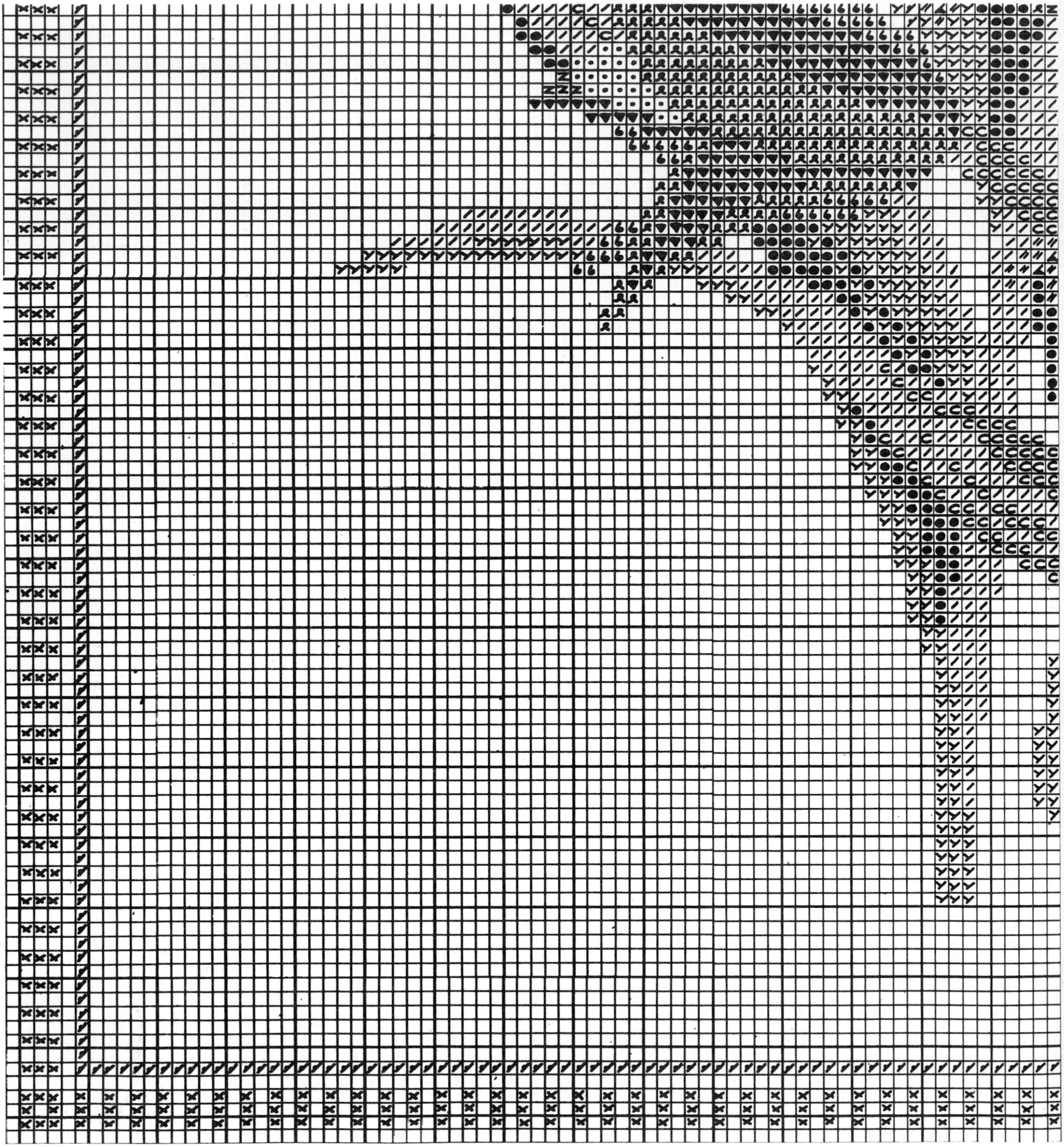

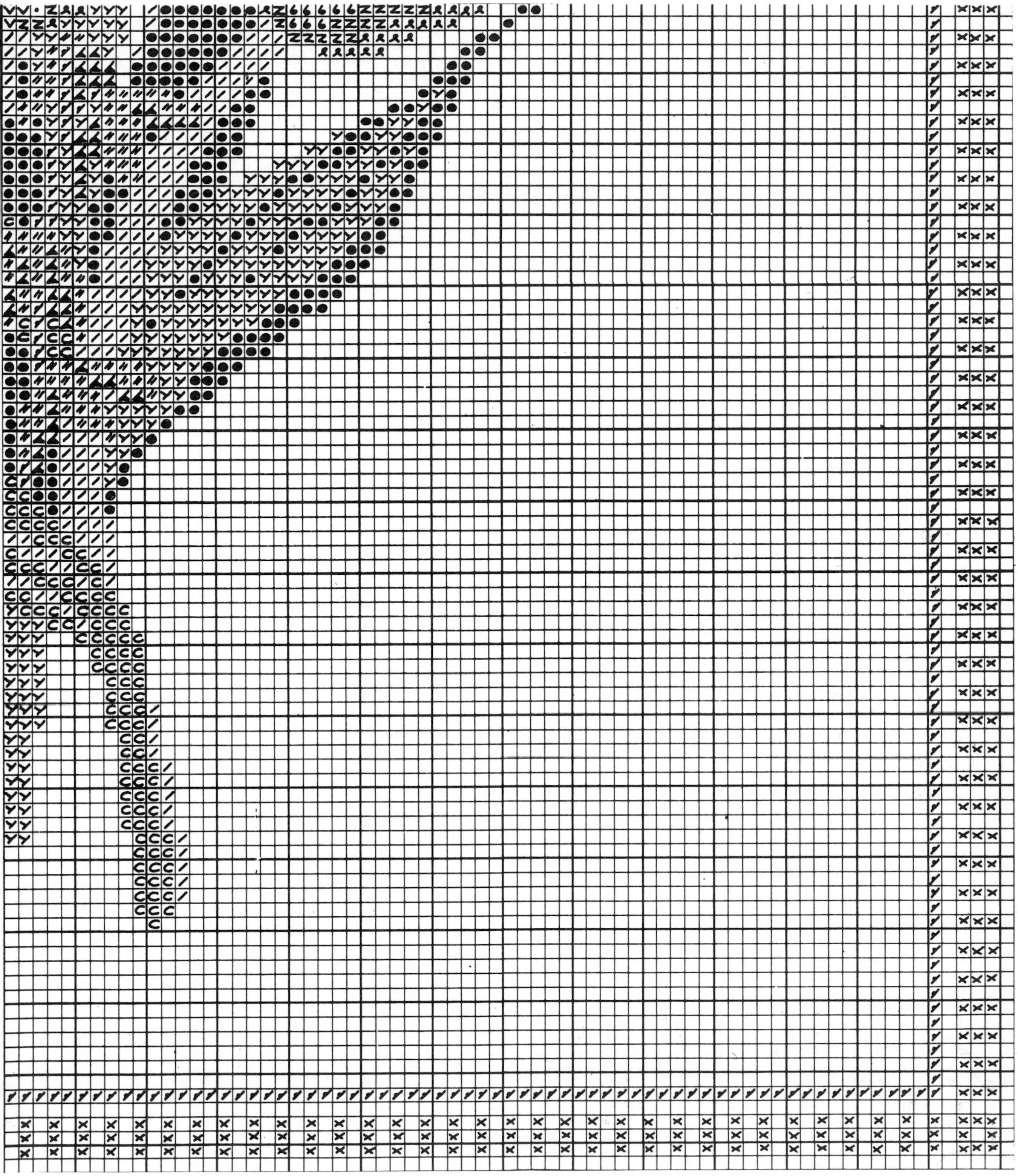

✕✕ SPRINGTIME CLOTH

See Plate 2.

Finished size: 15 × 15″ (38 × 38 cm.)
Cutting size: 18 × 18″ (45 × 45 cm.)

Materials

Linen with 25 threads/in. (10/cm.)
DMC embroidery yarn, one skein of each color

Instructions

Find the center of the fabric and of the design; the graph shows one-quarter of the design. Count out to the edge of the embroidery and begin stitching, using 2 strands of yarn in the needle. Press the finished embroidery. Where the cross stitches in the border are straight, count 25 threads outside of them; at the curved edges measure as much fabric as is equal to 25 threads. Cut away the surplus fabric. To hem, fold over 5 and then 10 threads to the wrong side and sew with small stitches.

DMC yarn

◼	310	black
◥	946	orange
3	972	dark yellow
╱	973	medium yellow
⬎	335	dark rose
Z	3326	medium rose
•	776	light rose
6	552	dark lilac
Ø	553	medium lilac
C	554	light lilac
✕	700	bright green
⸫	581	olive
╱	3345	dark green
Y	905	medium green
V	906	light green
∿	946	orange (backstitches)

SPRINGTIME CLOTH

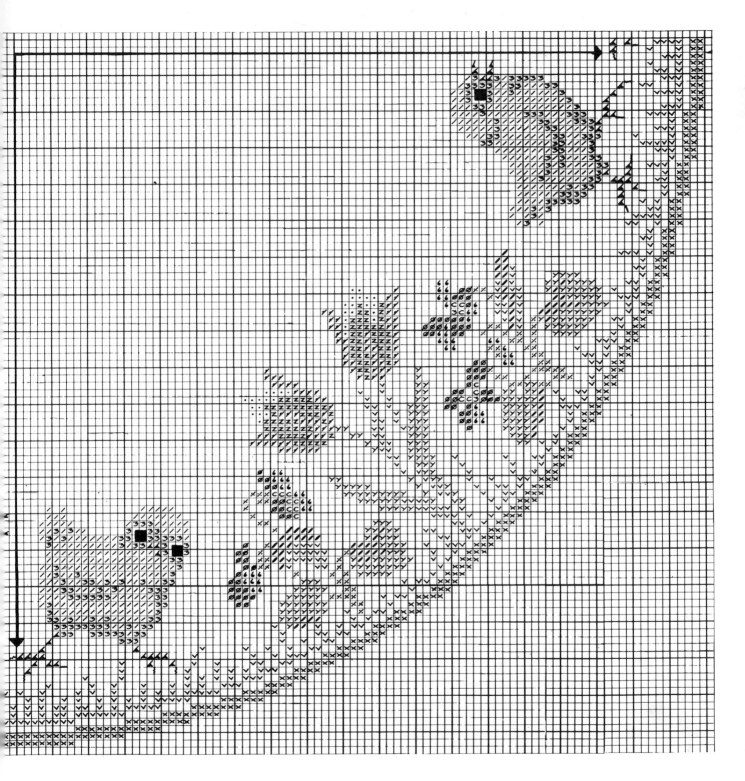

✕✕ WALLHANGING WITH PURPLE TULIPS
AND APPLEBLOSSOM

See Plate 3.

Finished size: 11 × 13″ (28 × 32 cm.)
Cutting size: 6 × 20″ (40 × 50 cm.)

Materials

Linen with 25 threads/in. (10/cm.)
DMC embroidery yarn, one skein of each color
One brass or bamboo fitting, approximately 12″ (30 cm.)

Instructions

Find the center of the fabric and of the design. Begin embroidering at the center, using 2 strands of yarn in the needle. To work the border, see the graphs on pages 18–19. Press the finished embroidery. For hemming and mounting instructions, see page 17.

DMC *yarn*

◤	891	dark red	☰	420	medium brown (+ border)
▽	893	medium red	✕	832	gold (+ border)
↗	894	light red	●	310	black
C	776	lightest red	▼	937	dark yellow-green
•	819	pale rose	Z	581	medium yellow-green
6	550	dark lilac	╱	471	light yellow-green
∥	552	medium lilac	⚲	986	dark green
⁎	553	light lilac	╋	988	medium green
V	209	light blue-lilac	∧	989	light green
⸪	210	lightest blue-lilac	⦰	307	yellow
◿	610	dark brown			

WALLHANGING WITH PURPLE TULIPS AND APPLEBLOSSOM

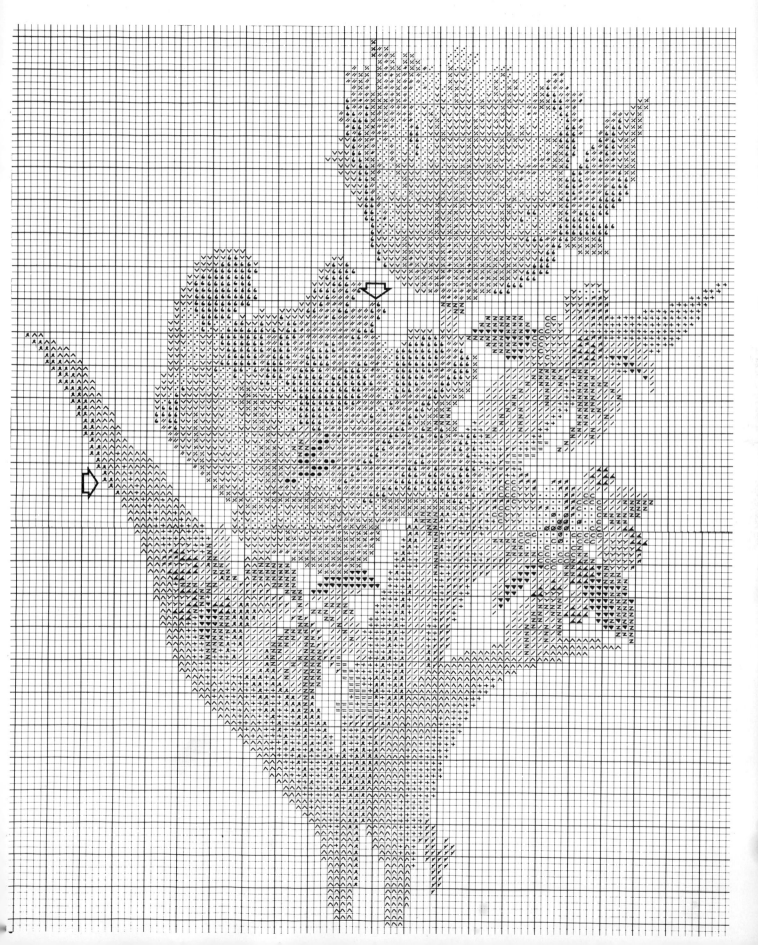

✕✕ STARFLOWER PLACEMAT

See Plate 4.

Finished size: 15 × 19″ (37 × 47 cm.)
Cutting size: 17 × 21″ (42 × 52 cm.)

Materials

Linen with 25 threads/in. (10/cm.)
DMC embroidery yarn (see color chart below for quantities)

Instructions

Begin embroidering 25 threads from the upper-left-hand corner. Use 2 strands of yarn in the needle. Press the finished embroidery and cut away surplus fabric so that only 25 threads are left on all four sides of the placemat. To hem, fold over 5 threads and then 10 threads to the wrong side and sew with small stitches.

DMC yarn

3021	dark brown (1 skein)
906	green (2 skeins)
972	yellow (1 skein)

STARFLOWER PLACEMAT

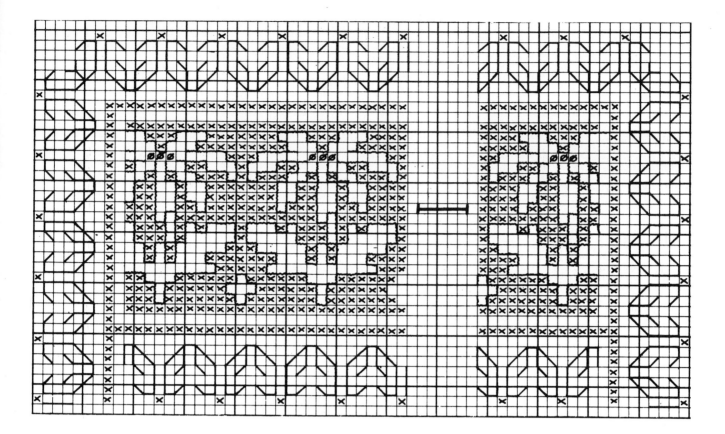

✕✕ NAPKINHOLDER WITH GEESE

See Plate 5.

Finished size: 11 × 12½″ (27 × 31 cm.); folded, 11 × 4½″ (27 × 11 cm.)
Cutting size: 13 × 14½″ (32 × 36 cm.)

Materials

Linen with 25 threads/in. (10/cm.)
DMC embroidery yarn, one skein of each color

Instructions

Begin embroidering the motif 1½ inches (3 cm.) from the bottom edge and 1½ inches (3 cm.) from the side. Use 2 strands of yarn in the needle. Embroider the motif on one short side only, but stitch the border all around. Press the finished embroidery. To hem, fold over 5 threads and then 10 threads to the wrong side and sew with small stitches. Fold the finished piece in three parts to form the napkinholder, with the geese on top as shown in Plate 5. Sew the two underneath parts together so that you have an envelope to put the napkin in.

NAPKINHOLDER WITH GEESE

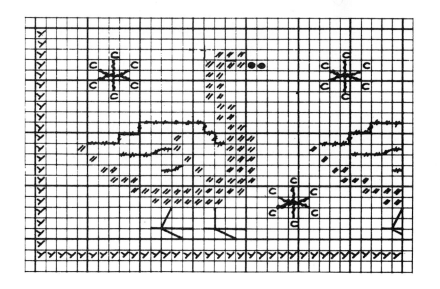

DMC yarn

Y	3347	green
//	921	rust (+ backstitches)
●	315	dark gray-lilac (+ backstitches)
C	676	yellow (+ backstitches)

⠿ PINK TULIPS WALLHANGING

See Plate 6.

Finished size: 11 × 13″ (28 × 32 cm.)
Cutting size: 16 × 20″ (40 × 50 cm.)

Materials

Linen with 25 threads/in. (10/cm.)
DMC embroidery yarn, one skein of each color
One brass or bamboo fitting, approximately 12″ (30 cm.)

Instructions

Find the center of the fabric and of the design. Begin embroidering at the center, using 2 strands of yarn in the needle. To work the border, see the graphs on pages 18–19. Press the finished embroidery. For hemming and mounting instructions, see page 17.

DMC yarn

Symbol	Number	Color
●	986	dark green
Z	987	medium green
∴	320	light green
╱	368	lightest green
3	470	medium yellow-green
↗	471	light yellow-green
∅	725	yellow
6	208	dark lilac
Y	209	medium lilac
C	211	light lilac
▼	309	darkest red
⚇	892	dark red
∥	893	medium red
V	894	light red
•	776	lightest red
◢	420	brown (+ border)
⊠	832	golden (+ border)

PINK TULIPS WALLHANGING

✕✕ YELLOW-WREATHED TABLECLOTH WITH
✕✕ DAFFODILS, TULIPS, AND FORSYTHIA

See Plate 7.

Finished cloth size: 56 × 56" (140 × 140 cm.)
Cutting size: 60 × 60" (150 × 150 cm.)
Embroidery measures: 20½" diameter (51 cm.)

Materials

Linen with 25 threads/in. (10/cm.)
DMC embroidery yarn (see color chart below for quantities)

Instructions

The graphs for this project show one-half of the design; the top of the second graph continues where the first graph left off at the bottom. Find the center of the fabric and the center of the design, count out to one of the flowers, and begin embroidering. Use 2 strands of yarn in the needle. When the embroidery is finished, measure 16½" (41 cm.) from the outermost cross stitch and stitch a border using DMC 732, light olive. Press the embroidery. Count 58 threads from the border and cut away surplus fabric. Fold over 10 and then 24 threads to the wrong side and sew with small stitches.

DMC yarn

H	3011	dark faded green (1 skein)
L	3012	medium faded green (1 skein)
■	935	darkest green (2 skeins)
●	367	dark green (2 skeins)
✕	320	medium green (2 skeins)
◹	368	light green (2 skeins)
∴	3348	lighter green (2 skeins)
⟋	783	light brown (1 skein)
⟋	972	orange (1 skein)
⊠	307	dark yellow (2 skeins)

•′	445	medium yellow (2 skeins)
•	727	light yellow (2 skeins)
⟋	444	light orange (2 skeins)
I	726	light yellow-brown (1 skein)
▼	351	dark red (1 skein)
6	350	light red (1 skein)
◣	327	dark lilac (1 skein)
⟋	451	dark gray (1 skein)
	732	light olive, for border (1 skein)

Plate 1. Wallhanging with Yellow Tulips

Plate 2. Springtime Cloth

Plate 3. Wallhanging
with Purple Tulips and Appleblossom

Plate 4. Starflower Placemat

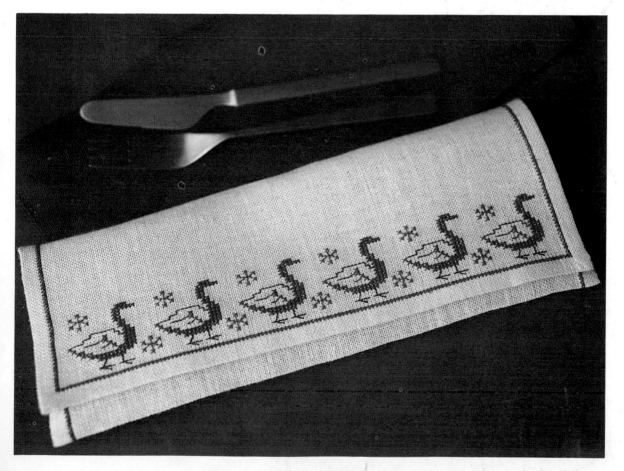

Plate 5. Napkinholder with Geese

Plate 6. Pink Tulips Wallhanging

Plate 7. Yellow-Wreathed Tablecloth with Daffodils, Tulips, and Forsythia

Plate 8. Cloth with Chamomile and Poppies

Plate 9. Wallhanging with a Sprig of Hairy Greenwood

Plate 10. Shelf Border
with Bluebell Motif

Plate 11. Rosebud Bookmark

Plate 12. Bellflower Table Runner

Plate 13. Pansy Pillow

Plate 14. Placemat and Plate Liner with Bluebells

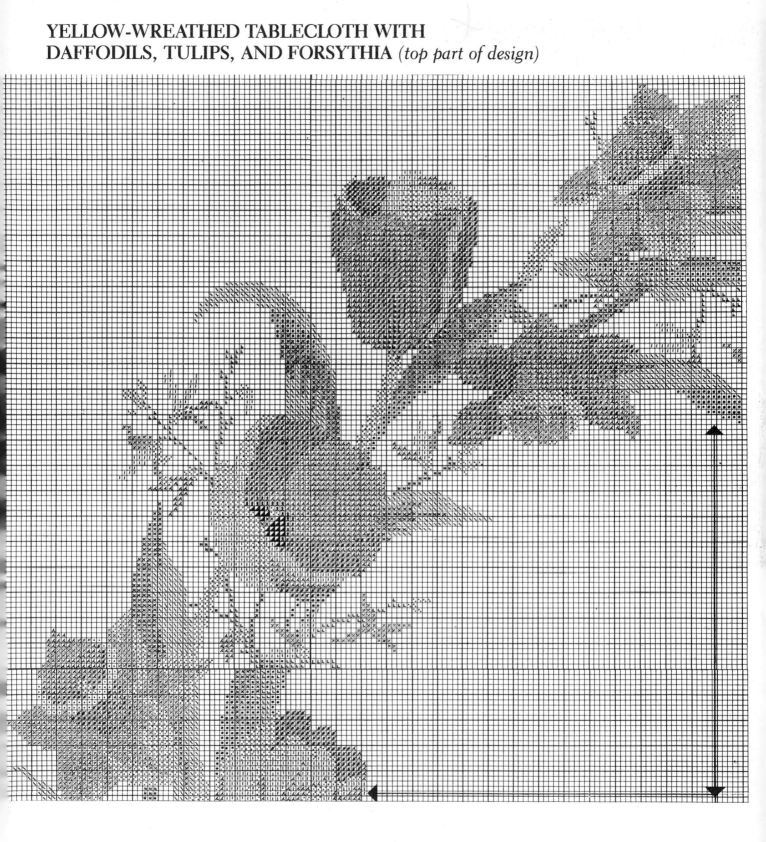

Summer

✕✕ CLOTH WITH CHAMOMILE AND POPPIES

See Plate 8.

Finished size: 22½ × 22½″ (56 × 56 cm.)
Cutting size: 24 × 24″ (60 × 60 cm.)

Materials

Linen with 25 threads/in. (10/cm.), in beige
DMC embroidery yarn, one skein of each color
White Pearl Cotton yarn, no. 8

Instructions

Find the center of the fabric and the design; the graphs show one-half of the design. Count out to the embroidery from the center. Stitch with 2 strands of DMC yarn in the needle, or, where it is used, 1 strand of white Pearl Cotton yarn. Press the finished embroidery. Count out 15 threads from the edge of the border and cut away surplus fabric. To hem, fold over 5 and then 10 threads to the wrong side of the work and sew with small stitches.

DMC yarn

935	dark green
937	dark yellow-green
470	medium yellow-green
471	light yellow-green
988	medium green (+ backstitches)
386	light green
731	olive
310	black
327	lilac

349	dark red
351	medium red
352	light red
972	orange
444	yellow
798	dark blue
799	medium blue
809	light blue
white	Pearl Cotton

CLOTH WITH CHAMOMILE AND POPPIES

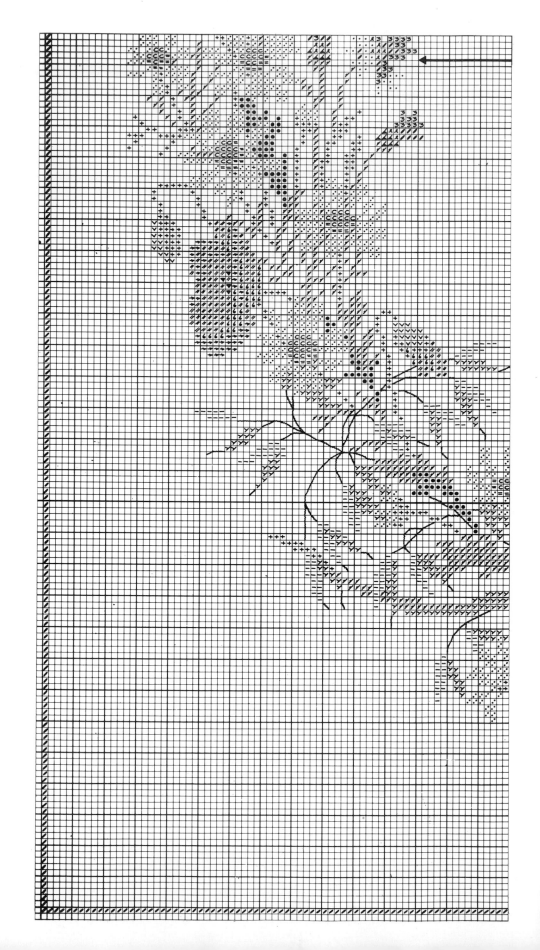

39

⚒ WALLHANGING WITH A SPRIG OF HAIRY GREENWOOD

See Plate 9.

Finished size: 9 × 12″ (23 × 30 cm.)
Cutting size: 11 × 14″ (28 × 35 cm.)

Materials

Linen with 25 threads/in. (10/cm.)
DMC embroidery yarn, one skein of each color
One brass or bamboo fitting, approximately 9½″ (24 cm.)

Instructions

Find the center of the embroidery and of the design and begin embroidering. Use 2 strands of yarn in the needle. The border (see small graph) should be stitched 24 threads from the top and bottom edges of the motif and 42 threads from its sides. Press the finished embroidery. For hemming and mounting instructions, see page 17.

DMC *yarn*

𝟼	783	darkest yellow
∿	972	dark yellow (+ backstitches)
∅	725	medium yellow
C	973	light yellow
╱	611	brown
↗	3012	olive
▪	319	dark green
✕	3346	medium green
╱	3347	light green

WALLHANGING WITH A SPRIG OF HAIRY GREENWOOD

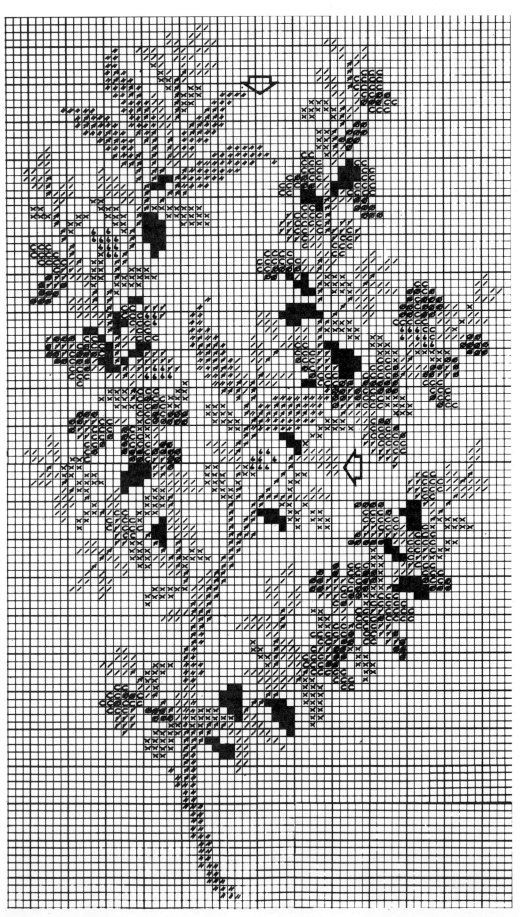

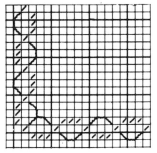

border

✕✕ SHELF BORDER WITH BLUEBELL MOTIF

See Plate 10.

Finished size: 2″ (5 cm.) deep and as long as your shelf
Cutting size: 3″ (6.50 cm.) deep

Materials

Linen with 25 threads/in. (10/cm.)
DMC embroidery yarn, one skein of each color
One piece of medium-weight interfacing, such as Pellon® nonwoven
    bonded textiles, the same size as the finished embroidery

Instructions

Stitch the motif according to the graph, using 2 strands of yarn in the needle. Press the finished embroidery. Place the interfacing on top of the wrong side, turn the edges of the linen to the back, and sew together with small stitches. This will help keep the shelf border stiff. Glue it to the edge of your kitchen shelf for a summery decoration.

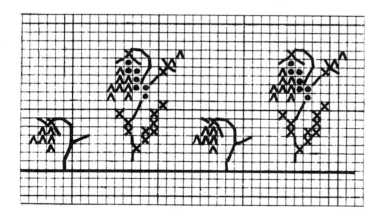

DMC *yarn*

●	798 medium blue
△	799 light blue
✕ / —	906 green (+ backstitches)

✕✕ ROSEBUD BOOKMARK

See Plate 11.

Finished size: 1¼ × 7″ (3 × 18 cm.); includes 1″ (2.5 cm.) fringe at each end
Cutting size: 2½ × 7″ (6 × 18 cm.)

Materials

Linen with 25 threads/in. (10/cm.)
DMC embroidery yarn, one skein of each color

Instructions

Fold the linen lengthwise in half to find the middle. Begin embroidering the motif 1″ (2.5 cm.) from the top, using 2 strands of yarn in the needle. Stitch three full motifs and red borders as shown in Plate 11. To hem, fold the linen over to the wrong side 2 threads from the red borders and cut away surplus fabric; sew together with small stitches. Make a 1″ (2.5 cm.) fringe on each end, as shown, by unraveling the linen.

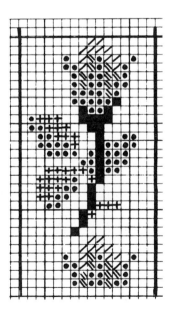

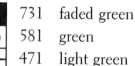

DMC yarn

■	731	faded green
●	581	green
⊞	471	light green
◪	349	red
◺	351	light red

BELLFLOWER TABLE RUNNER *(top part of design; see page 48 for instructions)*

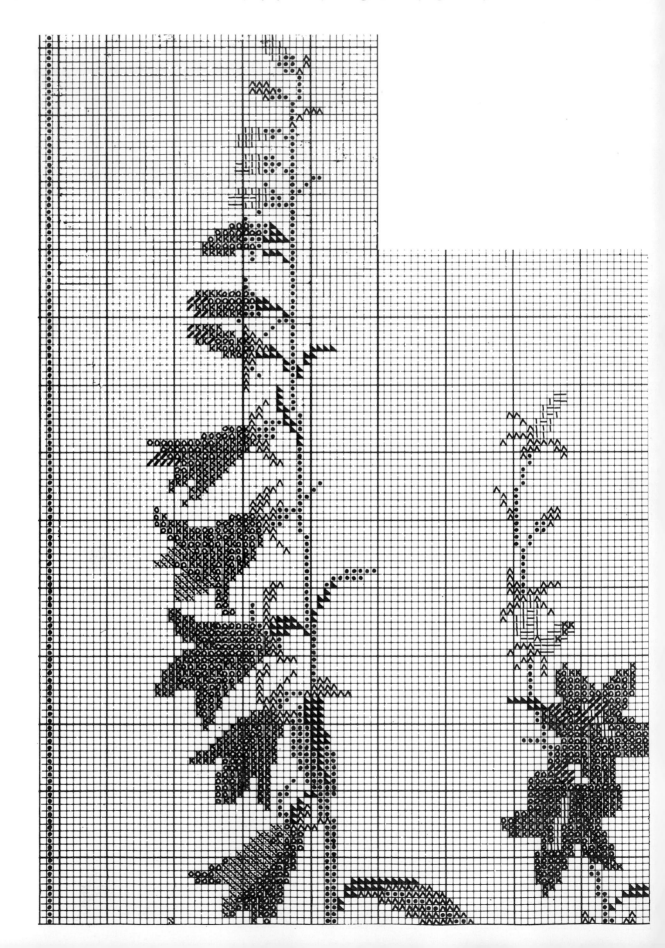

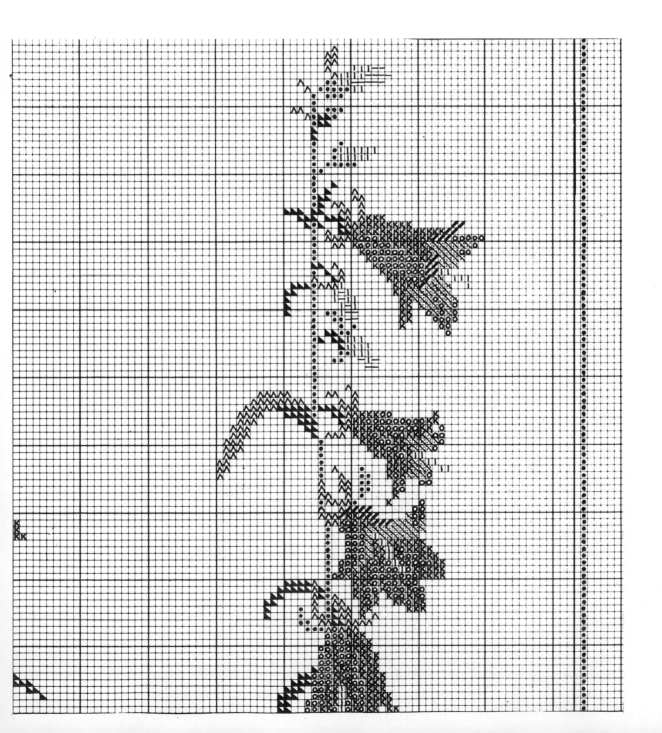

BELLFLOWER TABLE RUNNER *(bottom part of design)*

✕✕ BELLFLOWER TABLE RUNNER

See Plate 12.

Finished size: 13½ × 40″ (34 × 100 cm.)
Cutting size: 16 × 42″ (40 × 105 cm.)

Materials

Linen with 25 threads/in. (10/cm.)
DMC embroidery yarn, one skein of each color

Instructions

Begin by embroidering the border, starting 1″ (2.5 cm.) from both the top and the side of the fabric. Use 2 strands of yarn in the needle. Stitch the outer border in cross stitch and the inner border, four threads toward the inside, in backstitch. Place the flower motif in relation to the border according to the graph. Press the finished embroidery. To hem, fold over 5 threads and then 10 threads to the wrong side and sew with small stitches. One of the flower stems could also be used alone on a bellpull.

DMC yarn

	3051	dark green
	470	medium green
	471	light green
	3046	yellow-green
	327	blue-lilac
	550	dark lilac
	552	medium lilac
	553	light lilac
	210	gray-lilac
	554	rose

✂✂ PANSY PILLOW

See Plate 13.

Finished size: 14 × 14″ (35 × 35 cm.)
Cutting size: 16 × 16″ (40 × 40 cm.)

Materials

Linen with 25 threads/in. (10/cm.)
DMC embroidery yarn, one skein of each color
Linen for backing the pillow
Zipper, 14″ (35 cm.) long
Pillow form or loose stuffing

Instructions

Find the center of the fabric and of the design; the graph shows approximately one-half of the design. Count out to the edge of one of the flowers and begin embroidering. Use 2 strands of yarn in the needle. Count out 25 threads from the outside edge of the flowers and embroider the two borders (this distance has been shortened on the graph). Press the finished work. Place the embroidery against the fabric backing, right sides together, and sew along three of the sides. Turn the pillow casing right side out. Sew the zipper into the fourth side to make it easy to remove the pillow form or stuffing for cleaning.

DMC yarn

◣	3345	darkest green
—	3346	dark green
‖	3347	medium green
△	471	light green
◼	3371	earth
●	915	dark blue-red
≡	917	medium blue-red
∴	3687	light red
¦	3688	lightest red
▮	552	dark blue-lilac
◺	553	medium blue-lilac
+	210	light blue-lilac
◿	211	lightest blue-lilac
○	444	yellow
•	445	light yellow

✕✕ PLACEMAT AND PLATE LINER
✕✕ WITH BLUEBELLS

See Plate 14.

Finished size: placemat, 14 × 18″ (35 × 45 cm.); plate liner, 6 × 6″ (15 × 15 cm.)
Cutting size: placemat, 16 × 20″ (40 × 50 cm.); plate liner, 8 × 8″ (20 × 20 cm.)

Materials

Linen with 25 threads/in. (10/cm.)
DMC embroidery yarn, one skein of each color

Instructions

To work the placemat, begin embroidering 1 inch (2.5 cm.) in from the upper-left-hand corner for the border. Use 2 strands of yarn in the needle. Position the flowers according to the graph. Press the finished embroidery. Hem by folding the fabric over 5 and then 10 threads from the finished border and sewing with small stitches.

To work the plate liner, find the center of the fabric and of the design and begin embroidering. Use 2 strands of yarn in the needle. Press the finished embroidery. From the outside of the border count 21 threads and cut away surplus fabric. Fold over 4 and then 7 threads to the wrong side of the work and sew with small stitches. The plate liner is used between plates in an elegant table setting so they do not scratch each other.

For the placemat
DMC yarn

	3346	dark yellow-green
	3347	medium yellow-green (+ backstitches)
	471	light yellow-green
	3053	light green (+ backstitches)
	501	dark green
	320	medium green

	208	dark lilac
	792	dark blue
	793	medium blue
	809	light blue
	832	gold
	3042	light lilac

For the plate liner
DMC yarn

	501	dark green (+ backstitches)
	320	medium green
	733	light olive (+ backstitches)
	832	gold (+ backstitches)

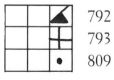

	792	dark blue
	793	medium blue
	809	light blue

PLACEMAT
WITH BLUEBELLS

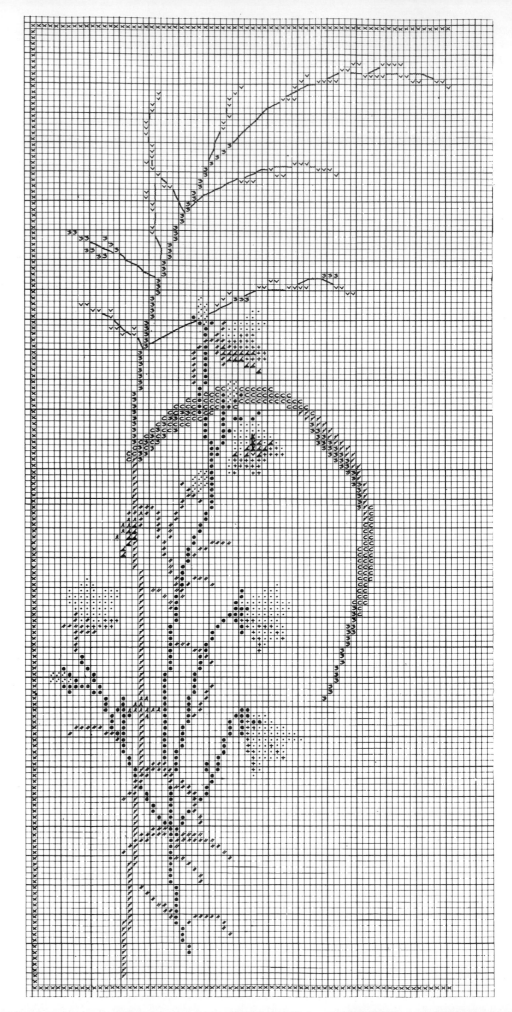

PLATE LINER WITH BLUEBELLS

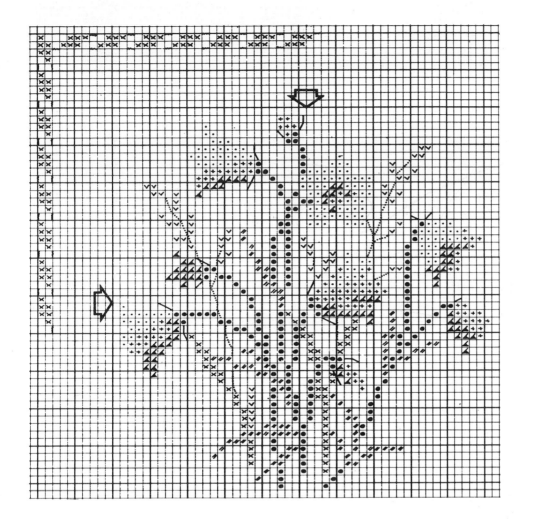

Fall

✂ AUTUMN CLOTH

See Plate 15.

Finished size: 16″ in diameter (40.5 cm.)
Cutting size: 18 × 18″ (45 × 45 cm.)

Materials

Linen with 25 threads/in. (10/cm.)
DMC embroidery yarn, one skein of each color

Instructions

Find the center of the fabric and of the design; the graph shows one-quarter of the design. Count out to the start of the embroidery and begin stitching there, using 2 strands of yarn in the needle. Press the finished embroidery. Count 25 threads from the outermost cross stitch in the border and cut away the surplus fabric. To hem, fold over 5 and then 10 threads to the wrong side and sew with small stitches.

DMC yarn

	3021	dark brown
	3345	dark green
	3346	medium green
	469	dark yellow-green
	581	medium yellow-green
	734	light yellow-green
	680	gold
	815	dark red
	326	medium red
	3328	light red

AUTUMN CLOTH

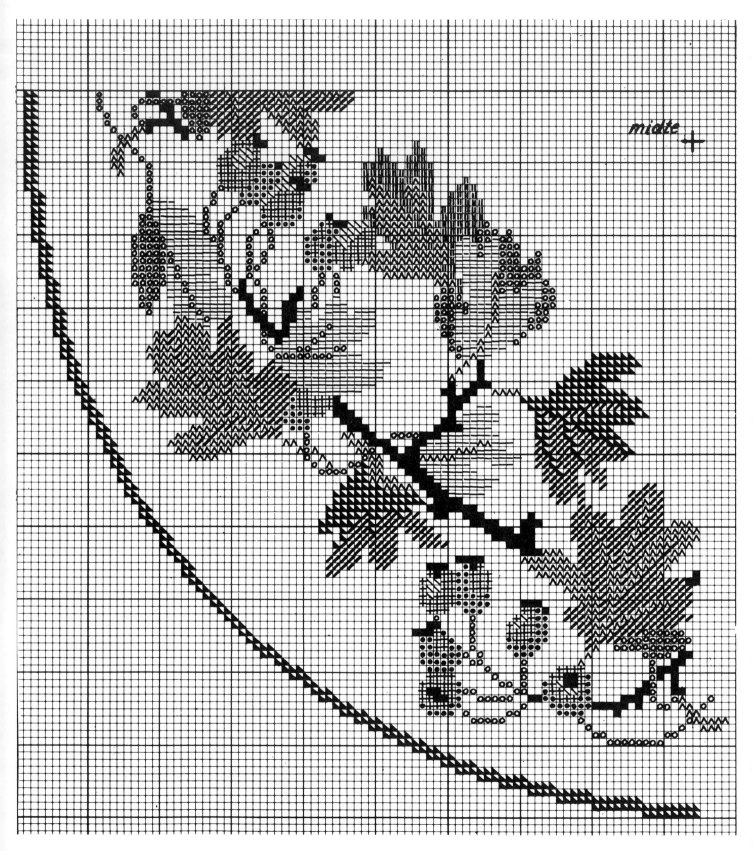

✂✂ LEAFY TABLE RUNNER

See Plate 16.

Finished size: 9 × 35″ (22 × 88 cm.)
Cutting size: 11 × 38″ (27 × 95 cm.)

Materials

Linen with 25 threads/in. (10/cm.)
DMC embroidery yarn, one skein of each color

Instructions

The graphs for this project show the lower half of the table runner. Find the center of the fabric and of the design, by following the arrows on the first graph until they intersect. Begin embroidering at the center, using 2 strands of yarn in the needle. To work the upper half of the runner, turn the linen 180° and work down from the center again (see Plate 16). Press the finished embroidery. Count out 33 threads from the outermost cross stitches on all sides and cut away surplus fabric. To hem, fold over 5 and then 12 threads to the wrong side of the work and hemstitch over 2 threads of fabric with DMC 729.

DMC yarn

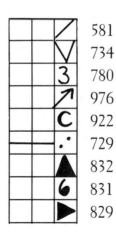

●	815	dark red
⟋	817	medium red
Z	349	red
Ø	946	orange
⟋	309	medium faded red
⟋	347	dark faded red
■	3021	dark brown
⟍	611	gray-brown
⊠	580	medium green

⟋	581	light green
⟍	734	light yellow-green
3	780	medium brown
↗	976	light brown
C	922	light red-brown
.·	729	gold (+ backstitches)
▲	832	medium olive
6	831	olive
▶	829	dark olive

LEAFY TABLE RUNNER

✕✕ PLATE LINER WITH A SPRIG
OF COTONEASTER

See Plate 17.

Finished size: 6 × 6″ (15.5 × 15.5 cm.)
Cutting size: 8 × 8″ (20 × 20 cm.)

Materials

Linen with 25 threads/in. (10/cm.)
DMC embroidery yarn, one skein of each color

Instructions

Find the center of the fabric and of the design and begin embroidering. Use 2 strands of
yarn in the needle. Press the finished work. To hem, fold over 4 and then 7 threads to the
wrong side and sew a hemstitch border over 2 threads. Plate liner motifs can be used in
other ways, such as in the corner of a placemat.

DMC yarn

610	gray-brown
975	red-brown
976	red
729	yellow
815	dark red
347	medium red
349	bright red
731	yellow-green
733	light green (+ backstitches and hemstitch border)

PLATE LINER WITH A SPRIG OF COTONEASTER

⁙ PLATE LINER WITH PRIVET MOTIF

See Plate 18.

Finished size: 6 × 6″ (15.5 × 15.5 cm.)
Cutting size: 8 × 8″ (20 × 20 cm.)

Materials

Linen with 25 threads/in. (10/cm.)
DMC embroidery yarn, one skein of each color

Instructions

Find the center of the fabric and of the design and begin embroidering. Use 2 strands of yarn in the needle. Press the finished work. Fold over 4 and then 7 threads to the wrong side and hemstitch the border over 2 threads.

DMC yarn

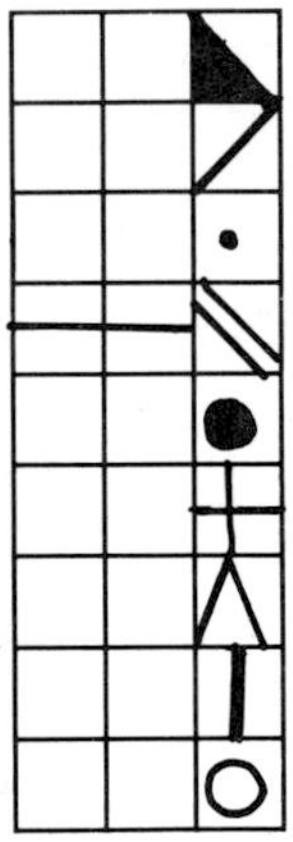

310	black
844	dark gray
647	light gray
640	gray-beige (+ hemstitch border)
3011	dark faded green
469	green
581	light green
830	golden brown
733	light yellow-green

Plate 15. Autumn Cloth

Plate 16. Leafy Table Runner

Plate 17. Plate Liner
with a Sprig of Cotoneaster

Plate 18. Plate Liner
with Privet Motif

Plate 19. Chestnut-Leaf Pillow

Plate 20. Placemat
with a Bough of Ash

Plate 21. Berry Plate Liner

Plate 22. Holiday Cloth

Plate 23. Wreath of Angels

Plate 24. Table Runner with Poinsettia

Plates 25 and 26. Plate Liners with Winter Motifs

Plate 27. Heralding Angel Bellpull

Plate 28. Advent Calendar

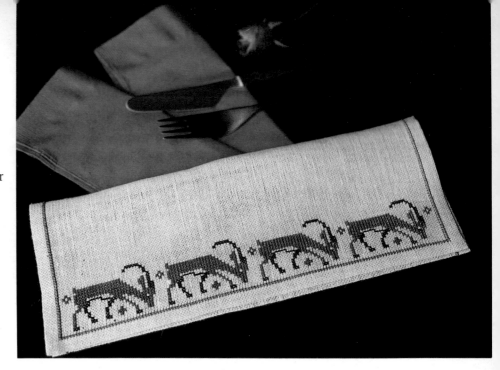

Plate 29. Napkinholder with Reindeer

Plate 30. Christmas Table Runner, Mother and Child

PLATE LINER WITH PRIVET MOTIF

✂✂ CHESTNUT-LEAF PILLOW

See Plate 19.

Finished size: 14 × 14″ (35.5 × 35.5 cm.)
Cutting size: 16 × 16″ (40 × 40 cm.)

Materials

Linen with 20 threads/in. (8/cm.)
DMC embroidery yarn (see color chart below for quantities)
Linen for backing
Zipper, 14″ (35 cm.) long
Pillow form or loose stuffing

Instructions

Find the center of the fabric and of the design. Begin embroidering at the center. Use 3 strands of yarn in the needle, covering 2 threads of fabric in each direction. Press the finished embroidery. Place the embroidery against the fabric backing, right sides together, and sew around three sides. Turn the pillow covering right side out. Sew the zipper into the fourth side to make it easy to remove the pillow form or stuffing for cleaning.

DMC yarn

■	3021	earth (1 skein)
●	347	dark red (1 skein)
‖	349	red (10 threads)
○	922	light rust (1 skein)
◫	832	yellow-green (1 skein)
◧	783	gold (1 skein)
△	725	yellow (1 skein)

PLACEMAT WITH A BOUGH OF ASH *(see page 70 for instructions)*

✕✕ PLACEMAT WITH A BOUGH OF ASH

See Plate 20.

Finished size: 14 × 18″ (35 × 45 cm.)
Cutting size: 16 × 20″ (40 × 50 cm.)

Materials

Linen with 25 threads/in. (10/cm.), in beige
DMC embroidery yarn, one skein of each color

Instructions

Find the middle of one long side of the fabric and of the design, which is indicated by the arrow at the top. Begin embroidering 30 threads from the top of the fabric. Use 2 strands of yarn in the needle. The border is stitched 2 threads from the outermost cross stitch of the motif and 25 threads from the edge of the three other sides. Press the finished embroidery. Cut away surplus fabric, leaving enough to fold over 5 threads and then 10 for the hem. Sew the hem with small stitches.

DMC yarn

3021	dark brown
975	medium red-brown
976	light red-brown (+ backstitches)
3078	light yellow
white	
680	dark beige (+ backstitches)
347	red (+ backstitches)
921	rust
732	green
676	beige

✕✕ BERRY PLATE LINER

See Plate 21.

Finished size: 6 × 6″ (15.5 × 15.5 cm.)
Cutting size: 8 × 8″ (20 × 20 cm.)

Materials

Linen with 25 threads/in. (10/cm.)
DMC embroidery yarn, one skein of each color

Instructions

Find the center of the fabric and of the design and begin embroidering. Use 2 strands of yarn in the needle. Press the finished work. To hem, fold over 4 and then 7 threads to the wrong side and hemstitch the border over 2 threads.

DMC yarn

○ 829	faded green (+ backstitches and hemstitch border)
◤ 938	dark brown
◥ 902	darkest red
‖ 221	dark faded red
● 815	dark fresh red
◿ 347	medium fresh red
∧ 349	bright red
— 760	rose

BERRY PLATE LINER

Winter

✂✂ HOLIDAY CLOTH

See Plate 22.

Finished size: 16½ × 16½″ (41 × 41 cm.)
Cutting size: 20 × 20″ (50 × 50 cm.)

Materials

Linen with 25 threads/in. (10/cm.)
DMC embroidery yarn (see color chart below for quantities)

Instructions

Find the center of the fabric, which corresponds to the square indicated by the arrow on the graph (the graph shows one-quarter of the design), and begin embroidering. Use 2 strands of yarn in the needle. Press the finished work. Count 25 threads from the border and cut away surplus fabric. To hem, fold over 5 and then 10 threads to the wrong side and sew with small stitches.

DMC yarn

310	black (backstitch) (1 skein)
900	red (1 skein)
731	brown (1 skein)
906	light green (2 skeins)
905	medium green (2 skeins)
904	dark green (2 skeins)
580	faded green (1 skein)
972	yellow (+ backstitches) (1 skein)
444	light yellow (1 skein)

✕✕ WREATH OF ANGELS

See Plate 23.

Finished size: 15″ diameter (38 cm.)
Cutting size: 18 × 18″ (45 × 45 cm.)

Materials

Linen with 30 threads/in. (12/cm.)
DMC embroidery yarn, one skein of each color
Gold thread, DMC Fil d'or, one roll

Instructions

Find the center of the fabric and of the design (where the arrows intersect) and count out
to the start of one of the motifs. The graph shows one-quarter of the design. Use 2 strands
of yarn in the needle; where the color chart indicates that gold thread should be used as
well as yarn, use one strand of yarn and one of gold thread. Press the finished embroidery.
Count out 25 threads from the border and cut away surplus fabric. To hem, fold over 5
and then 10 threads to the wrong side of the work and sew with small stitches.

DMC yarn

833   gold (+ gold thread)
434   brown
951   flesh (+ gold thread)
989   green
946   orange (+ gold thread)

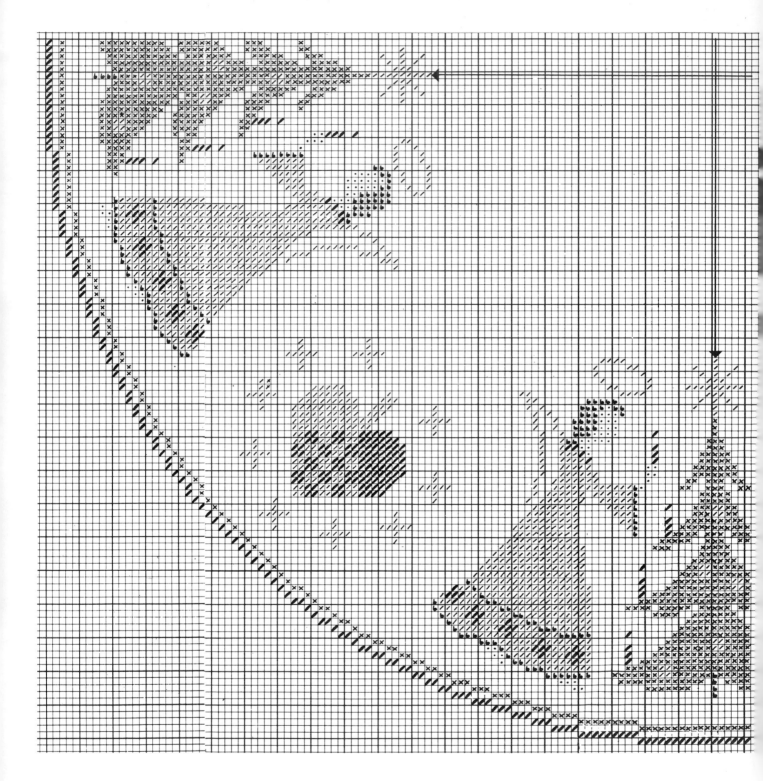

✖✖ TABLE RUNNER WITH POINSETTIA

See Plate 24.

Finished size: 11½ × 41½" (29 × 104 cm.)
Cutting size: 13½ × 44" (34 × 110 cm.)

Materials

Linen with 20 threads/in. (8/cm.)
DMC embroidery yarn (see color chart below for quantities)

Instructions

The graph for this project shows the three different flowers that are repeated along the length of the runner. Find the center of the fabric and of the design, by following the large arrows on the graph. Use 3 strands of yarn in the needle. Beginning at the center of the fabric, embroider down to the small arrow at the right side of the graph. Then return to the top of the graph and continue embroidering down to the bottom. You will have stitched the bottom half of the runner. Work the top half of the runner from the same graph, referring to Plate 24 to see how the motifs are repeated. Do not turn the graph or the fabric around. Press the finished embroidery. To hem, fold over 5 threads and then 8 threads to the wrong side and sew with small stitches.

DMC yarn

◢	892	light red (2 skeins)
=	891	medium red (3 skeins)
◿	349	dark red (2 skeins)
●	304	darkest red (2 skeins)
V	3064	light brown (1 skein)
⊘	832	yellow-brown (1 skein)
•	471	light yellow-green (1 skein)
↗	989	light green (2 skeins)
✕	988	medium green (1 skein)
6	987	dark green (1 skein)
.˙	503	light blue-green (1 skein)
3	502	medium blue-green (2 skeins)
⚵	501	dark blue-green (1 skein)
C	742	yellow (1 skein)

TABLE RUNNER
WITH POINSETTIA

✕✕ PLATE LINERS WITH WINTER MOTIFS

See Plates 25 and 26.

Finished size: 6 × 6″ (15 × 15 cm.)
Cutting size: 8 × 8″ (20 × 20 cm.)

Materials

Linen with 25 threads/in. (10/cm.)
DMC embroidery yarn, one skein of each color

Instructions

Find the center of the fabric and of the design. Begin embroidering at the center, using 2 strands of yarn in the needle. The graphs show approximately one-quarter of the design. Press the finished embroidery. Count 21 threads from the edge of the border and cut away the surplus fabric. To hem, fold over 5 and then 8 threads to the wrong side and sew with small stitches.

PLATE LINERS WITH WINTER MOTIFS

Motif with hearts
DMC yarn

—		911	blue-green (backstitches)
	V	906	green
～	X	349	red (+ backstitches)
	O	972	yellow

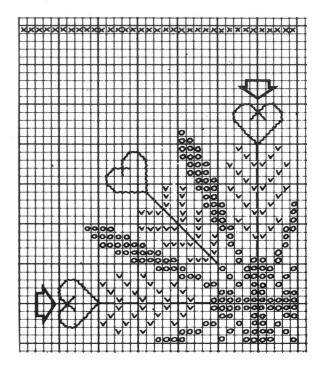

Motif with branches
DMC yarn

	6	904	dark green
	V	906	medium green
	/	907	light green
		900	orange
～	O	972	yellow (+ backstitches)

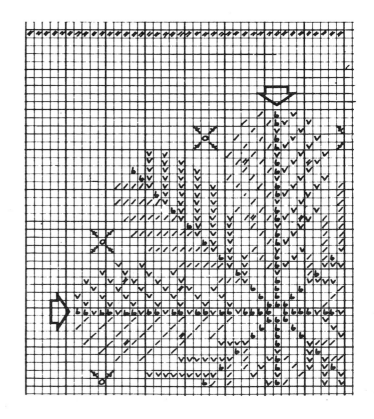

✕✕ HERALDING ANGEL BELLPULL

See Plate 27.

Finished size: 3⅛ × 13″ (8 × 33 cm.)
Cutting size: 8 × 16″ (20 × 40 cm.)

Materials

Linen with 25 threads/in. (10/cm.)
DMC embroidery yarn, one skein of each color
One piece of medium-weight interfacing, such as Pellon® nonwoven
    bonded textiles, 3⅛ × 13″ (8 × 33 cm.)
One brass bellpull fitting (available at needlework shops, or from The
    Counting House, Box 155, Pawleys Island, S.C. 29585)

Instructions

Fold the fabric in half lengthwise to find the middle. Measure 1⅜″ (3 cm.) from the top of the fabric and begin embroidering at the arrow on the graph. Use 2 strands of yarn in the needle. Press the finished embroidery. Place the interfacing on top of the wrong side of the work and fold the linen over 4 threads from the red border, around the interfacing. Sew with small stitches. At the top and bottom, make casings for the bellpull fitting and sew together.

DMC yarn

|	353	light flesh
+	352	dark flesh
6	518	dark blue
−	519	light blue
╱	433	dark brown
Z	415	gray
•	white	
↓	900	dark red
⊠	741	yellow
╱	972	light yellow
O	976	light brown

Note: The backstitches of the stars follow the colors of the cross stitches.

HERALDING ANGEL BELLPULL

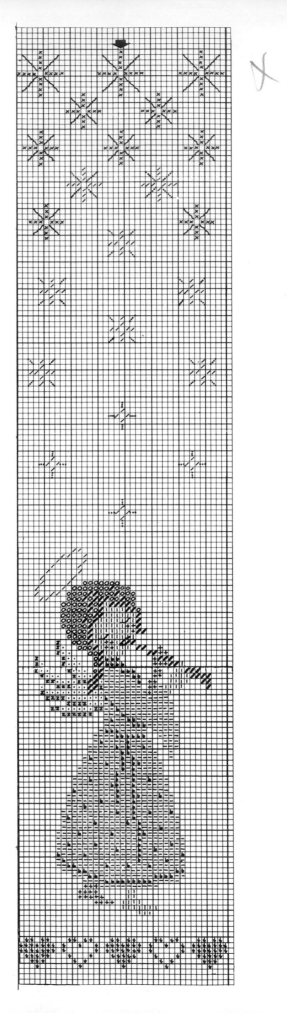

✗✗ ADVENT CALENDAR

See Plate 28.

Finished size: 18½ × 21½" (46 × 54 cm.)
Cutting size: 22 × 26" (55 × 65 cm.)

Materials

Linen with 20 threads/in. (8/cm.)
DMC embroidery yarn, 1 skein of each color
Medium-weight interfacing, such as Pellon® nonwoven bonded textiles,
    18½ × 21½" (46 × 54 cm.)
Linen for backing, the same size as the interfacing
Twenty-four red plastic rings
Two brass rings for hanging

Instructions

There are six graphs for this project, three for the top half of the design and three for the bottom. In the first two graphs, follow the arrows to find the center of the design. Find the center of the fabric and begin embroidering. Use 3 strands of yarn in the needle. Press the finished embroidery. With the embroidered side face down, lay the interfacing and the backing material on the linen. Turn back the edges of the linen over the sandwich of materials and cut away surplus fabric. Fold the edges of the linen over and sew it to the rest of the material with small stitches. Attach the twenty-four red plastic rings across the top as shown in Plate 28. Twenty-four small gift-wrapped packages should be tied onto the rings and opened, one each day, before Christmas.

DMC yarn

731	dark faded green	972	dark yellow
832	gold	444	light yellow
987	dark fresh green	434	medium brown
906	light fresh green	435	light brown
797	dark blue	436	lightest brown
798	light blue	352	dark rose
606	red	353	light rose
310	black		

ADVENT CALENDAR *(upper left and middle sections)*

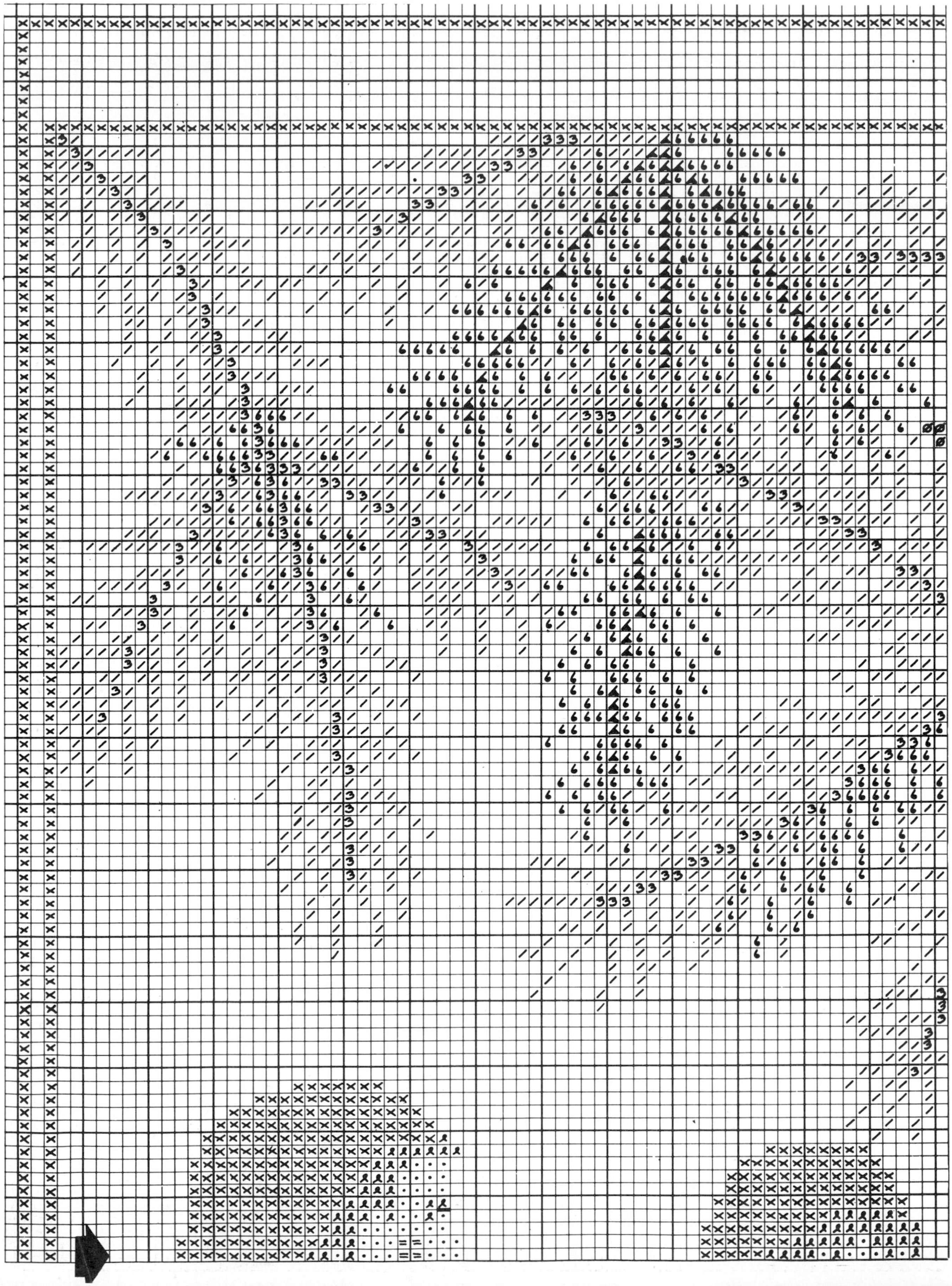

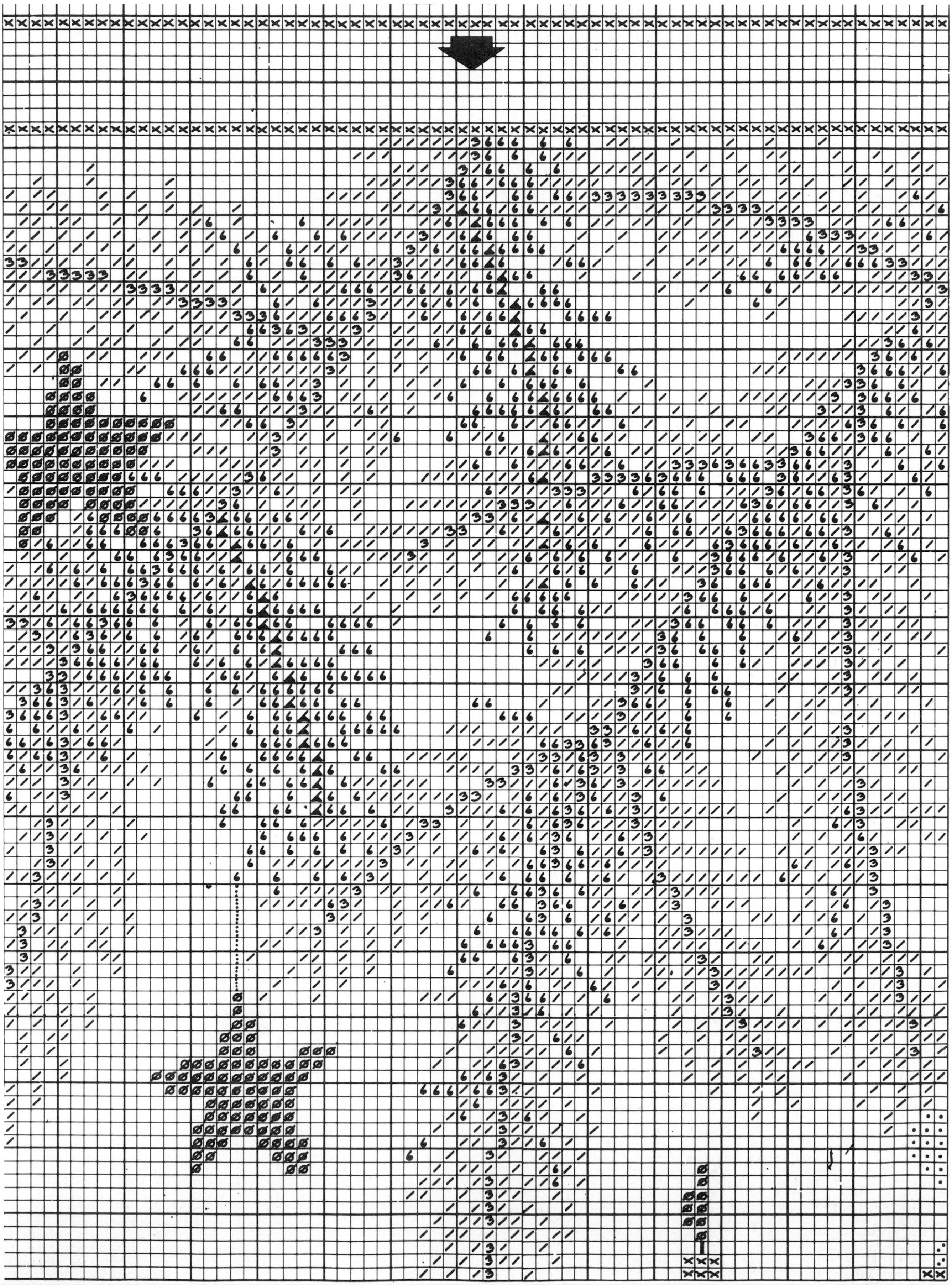

ADVENT CALENDAR *(upper right section)*

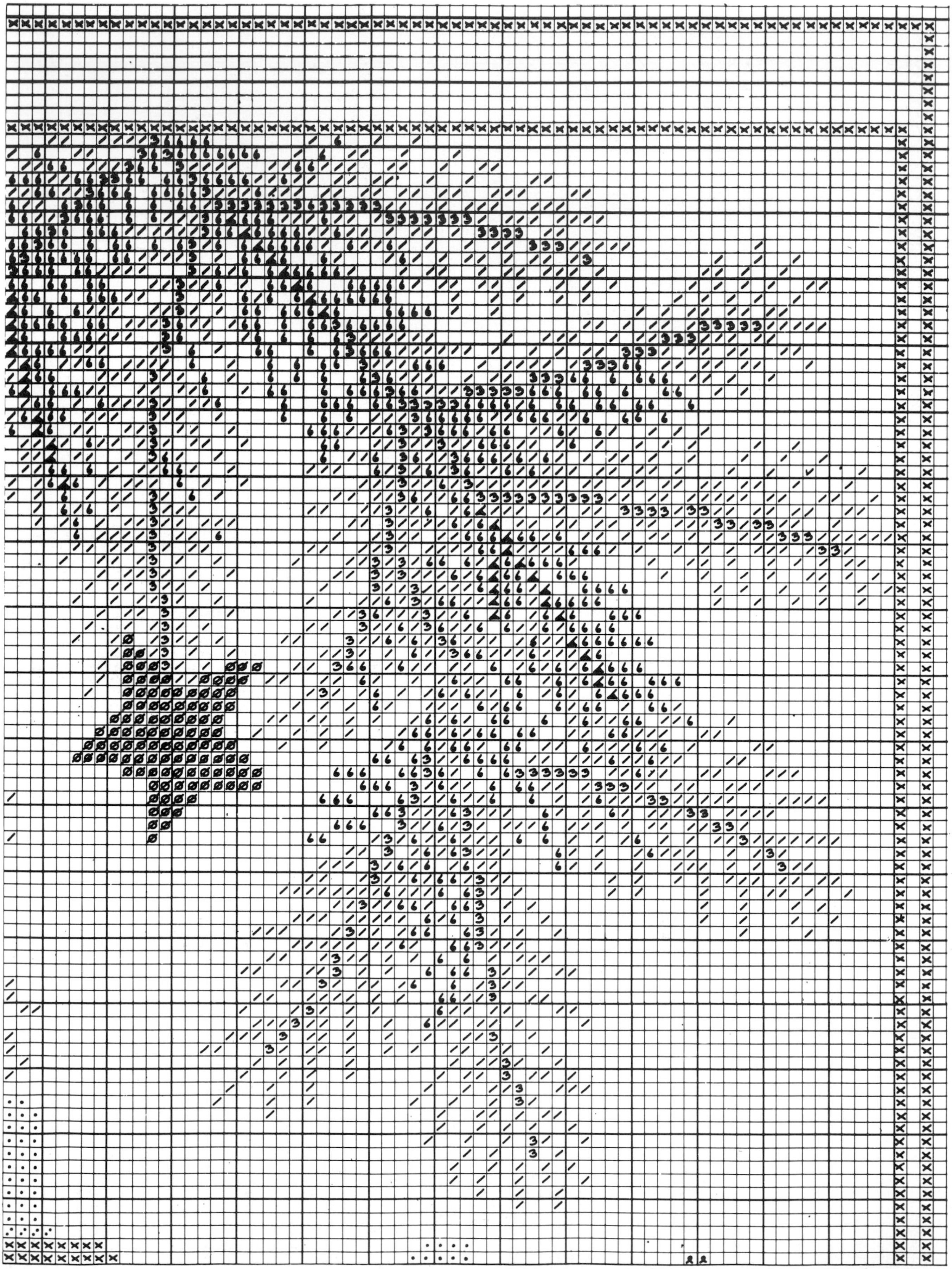

(lower left section)

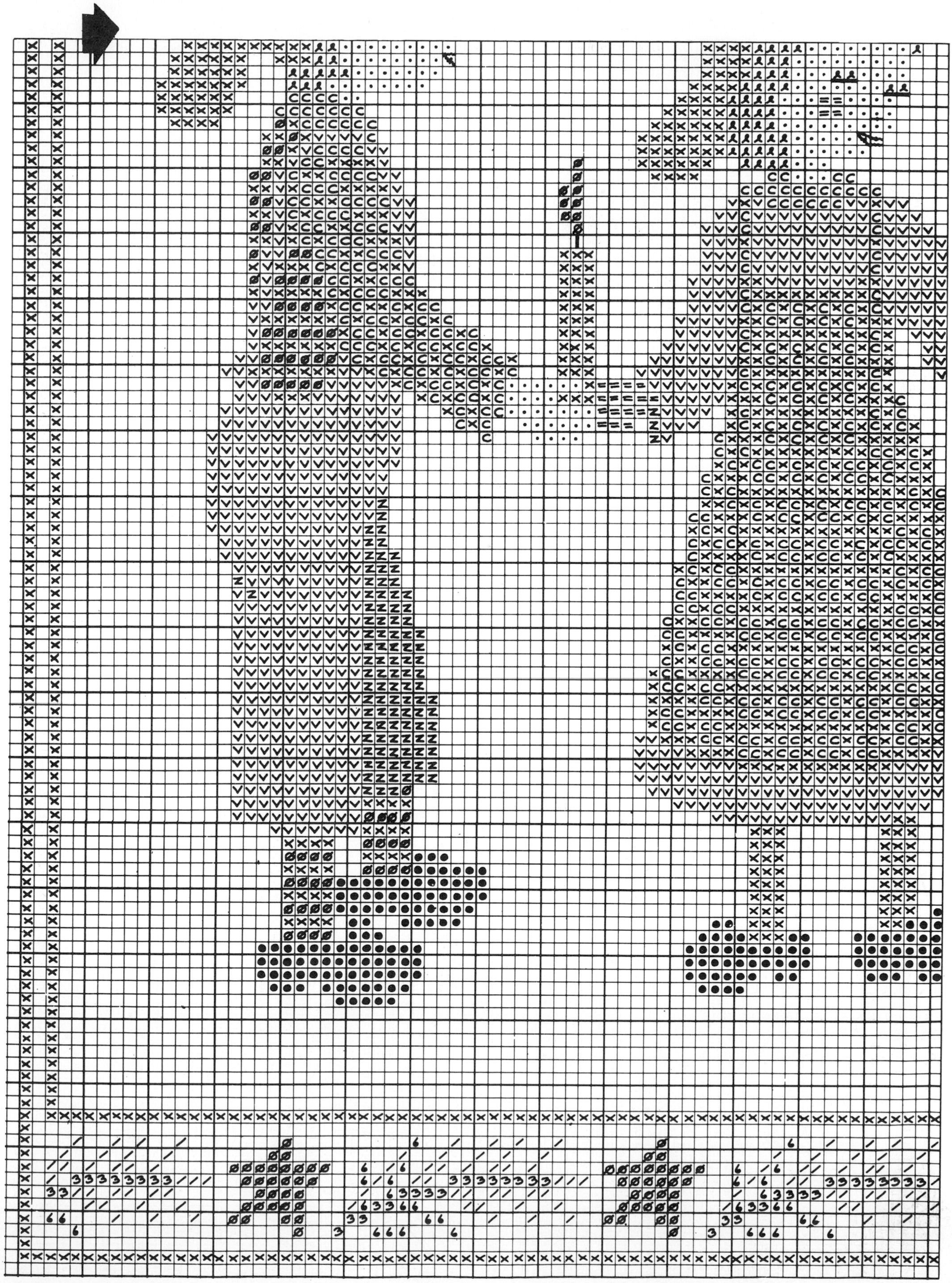

ADVENT CALENDAR *(lower middle and right sections)*

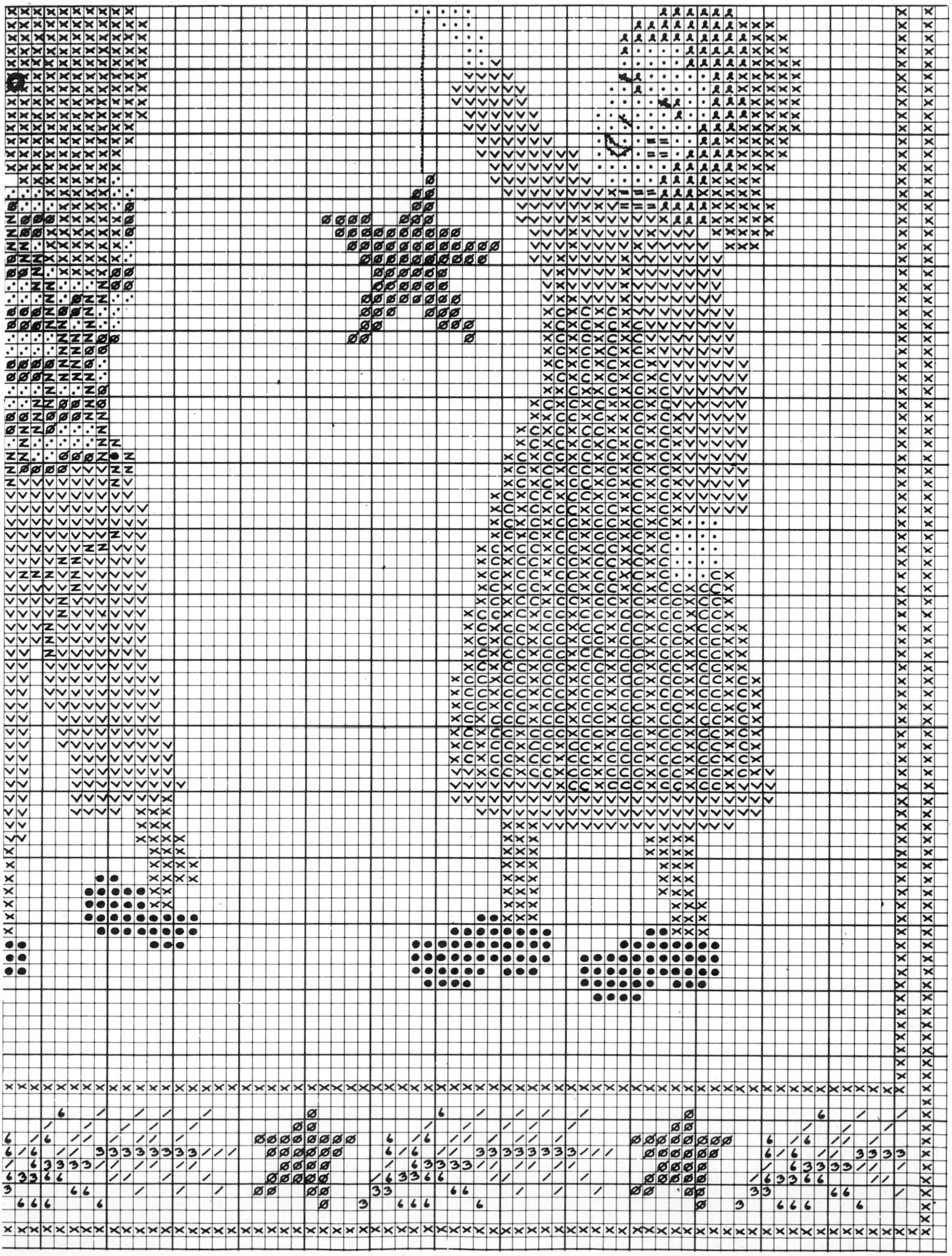

✕✕ NAPKINHOLDER WITH REINDEER
  ✕✕

See Plate 29.

Finished size:	11 × 12½″ (27 × 31 cm.)
Measurements when folded:	11 × 4½″ (27 × 11 cm.)
Cutting size:	13 × 14½″ (32 × 36 cm.)

Materials

Linen with 25 threads/in. (10/cm.)
DMC embroidery yarn, one skein of each color

Instructions

Begin embroidering the motif 1½ inches (3 cm.) from the bottom edge of the linen and 1½ inches (3 cm.) from the side. Use 2 strands of yarn in the needle. Stitch the motif only at the one short side; stitch the border all around. Press the finished embroidery. Count 25 threads from the border and cut away surplus fabric. To hem, fold over 5 threads and then 10 threads from the edge and sew with small stitches. Fold the embroidery in three parts so that the reindeer motif is on top (see Plate 29). Sew the bottom two parts together to form an envelope to put the napkin into.

NAPKINHOLDER WITH REINDEER

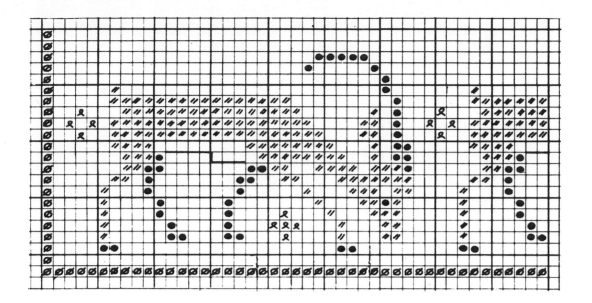

DMC *yarn*

╱╱		208	lilac
●		336	dark blue (+ backstitches)
ℛ		309	red
∅		597	turquoise

✕✕ CHRISTMAS TABLE RUNNER,
MOTHER AND CHILD

See Plate 30.

Finished size: 10 × 34″ (25 × 85 cm.)
Cutting size: 12 × 36″ (30 × 90 cm.)

Materials

Linen with 25 threads/in. (10/cm.)
DMC embroidery yarn (see color chart for quantities)

Instructions

Find the center of the fabric and of the motif, as shown by the arrow at the bottom of the graph. Count up to the top of the motif and begin embroidering. Use 2 strands of yarn in the needle. Press the finished work. To hem, fold over 5 and then 10 threads to the wrong side and sew with small stitches.

DMC yarn

—	310	black (+ backstitches) (2 skeins)
—	762	light gray (2 skeins)
•		white (8 skeins)
〜〜	433	brown (+ backstitches) (2 skeins)
—	781	gold (1 skein)
• • • ○	972	yellow (+ backstitches) (5 skeins)
╱	321	dark red (3 skeins)
‖	606	red (16 skeins)
∧	407	dark beige (1 skein)
╱	352	dark rose (1 skein)
│	353	light rose (2 skeins)
●	797	dark blue (5 skeins)
=	798	light blue (4 skeins)
+	553	dark lilac (3 skeins)
∴	210	light lilac (3 skeins)
╲	905	green (16 skeins)